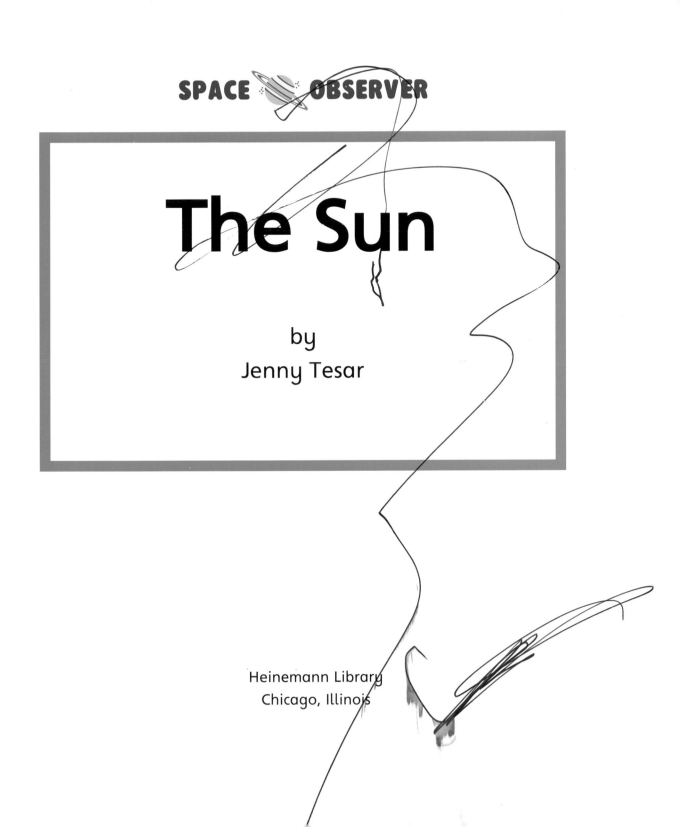

SPACE OBSERVER

The Sun

by
Jenny Tesar

Heinemann Library
Chicago, Illinois

© 1998 Reed Educational & Professional Publishing
Published by Heinemann Library,

Chicago, IL

Customer Service 888-454-2279
Visit our website at www.heinemannlibrary.com

04 03 02

10 9 8 7 6 5 4

ISBN 1-57572-582-7
Library of Congress Cataloging-in-Publication Data

Tesar, Jenny E.
    The Sun / by Jenny Tesar
        p. cm. — (Space Observer)
    Includes bibliographical references and index.
    Summary: Introduces the sun, discussing its surface, atmosphere, eclipses. birth, death, and place in the solar system.
    ISBN 1-57572-582-7 (lib. bdg.)
    1. Sun—Juvenile Literature. [1. Sun.] I. Title II. Series:
  Tesar, Jenny E.   Space Observer
  QB521.5.T47   1997
  523.7—dc21   97–25177
                                                     CIP
                                                     AC

Acknowledgments
The author and publishers are grateful to the following for permission to reproduce copyright photographs:
Page 4: ©NOAO/Science Photo Library/Photo Researchers, Inc.; page 5: Gazelle Technologies, Inc.; page 7: ©David A. Hardy/Science Photo Library/Photo Researchers, Inc.; page 8: ©Jisas/Lockheed/Science Photo Library/Photo Researchers, Inc.; page 9: ©Ton Kinsbergen/ESA/Science Photo Library/Photo Researchers, Inc.; page 10: ©Mark Marten/NASA/Photo Researchers, Inc.; pages 11, 22: ©Dennis Di Cicco/Peter Arnold, Inc.; pages 12-13: ©NASA; page 14: ©Jack Finch/SPL/Science Source/Photo Researchers, Inc.; page 15: ©Jack Finch/Science Photo Library/Photo Researchers, Inc.; page 16: ©Chromosohm/Sohn/Photo Researchers, Inc.; page 17: ©Jerry Schad/Photo Researchers, Inc.; pages 18–19: ©Will and Deni McIntyre/Photo Researchers, Inc.; page 20: PhotoDisc, Inc.; page 21: ©Blackbirch Press, Inc.; page 23: ©NASA/Photri.

Cover photograph: ©NOAO/Science Photo Library/Photo Researchers, Inc.

Every effort has been made to contact copyright holders of any material reproduced in this book. Any omissions will be rectified in subsequent printings if notice is given to the publisher.

Some words are shown in bold, **like this**. You can find out what they mean by looking in the glossary.

Printed by South China Printing in Hong Kong / China

Contents

What Is the Sun?

The Sun is a star. It is round like a ball. It is the closest star to Earth. It is 93 million miles away. If the Sun were hollow, it could hold more than 1 million Earths!

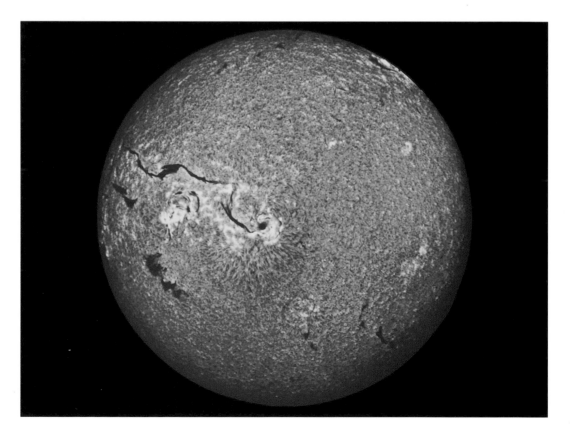

The Sun is 1 million times larger than Earth (shown above).

The next closest star is about 250,000 times farther away. Imagine the Sun as a basketball lying at one end of a football field. On the other end of the field is Earth, which is smaller than a gumball.

The Solar System

The Sun is at the center of our Solar System. Solar means "sun." The Solar System is made up of the Sun and everything that travels around it.

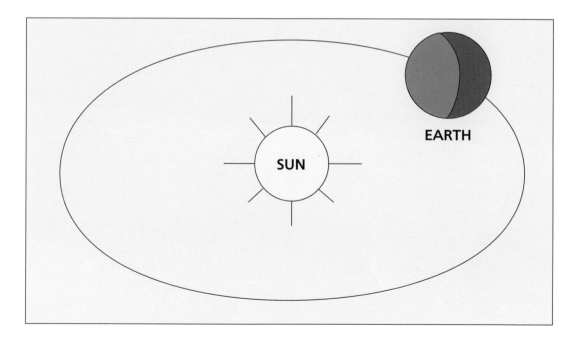

It takes Earth a year to travel around the Sun.

There are nine **planets**, including Earth, in the Solar System. It takes Earth one year to orbit, or travel around the Sun. There are many star systems like the Solar System in space.

Earth is one of nine planets that orbit around the Sun.

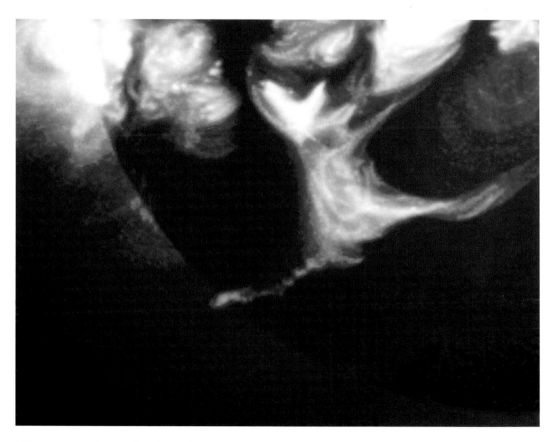

The Sun is a ball of hot gases.

The Sun is not **solid** like Earth. It is a ball of very hot gases. These gases give off **energy**.

8

Some of the energy from the Sun travels to Earth, to give us light and heat. This energy is so strong that it can burn our skin—even though it comes from 93 million miles away!

A space probe helps scientists study the Sun.

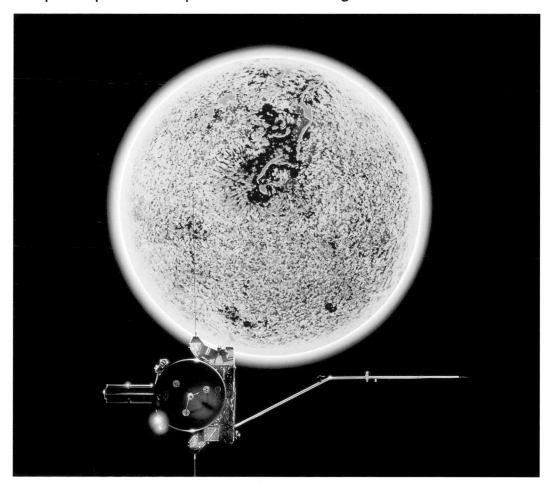

The Sun's Surface

The Sun's **surface** is always changing. Hot gases from deep inside the Sun rise to the surface. They make the surface bubble and boil.

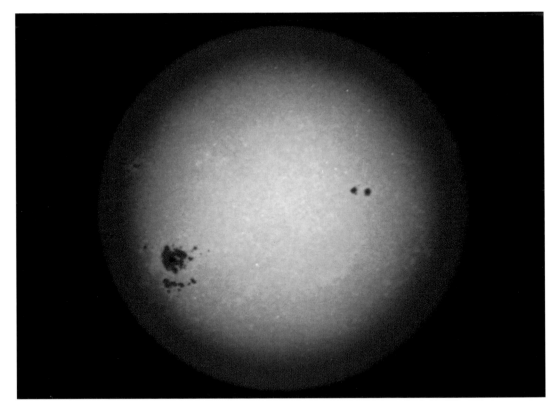

The dark spots on the sun are sunspots.

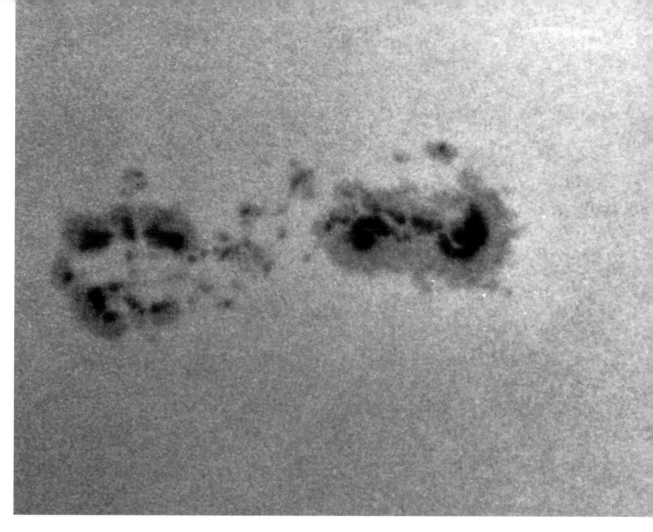

A sunspot can be as big as Earth.

There are sunspots, which are like dark spots on the surface of the Sun. Sunspots are darker because they are cooler than other parts of the Sun's surface.

The Sun's Atmosphere

The Sun is surrounded by a layer of gases called the **atmosphere**. The Sun's atmosphere spreads millions of miles into space.

Sometimes, ribbons and sheets of flaming gas shoot up through the Sun's atmosphere. They may travel out into space. Or they may loop around to make big arches over the Sun's **surface.**

Ribbons of burning gas can shoot through the Sun's atmosphere.

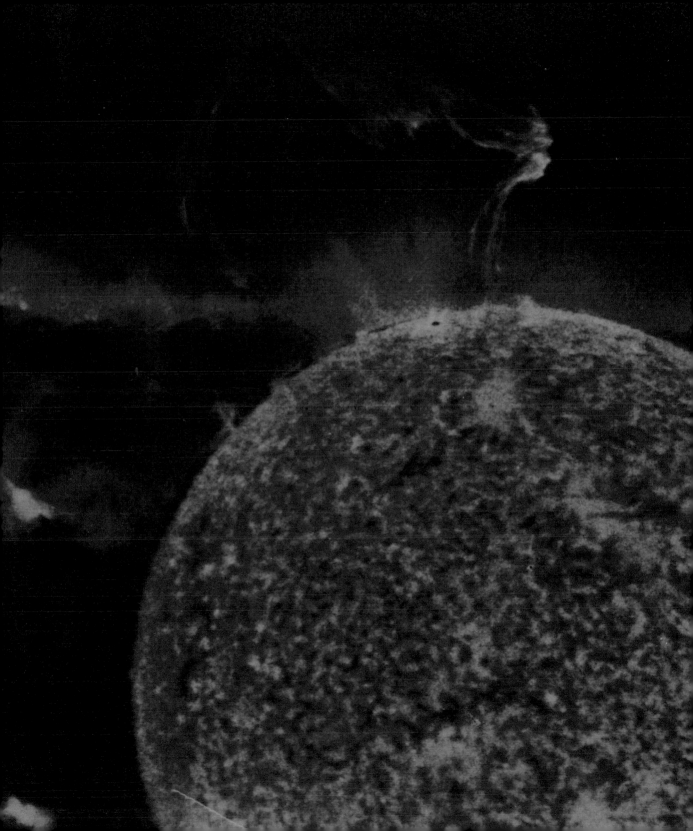

Solar Wind

The solar wind moves very fast away from the Sun. It reaches Earth traveling over 1 million miles per hour! That's more than 1,000 times faster than a giant jet airplane!

An aurora glows in the night sky.

Auroras are very bright near the North Pole
and the South Pole.

Sometimes, the solar wind causes a glow in
Earth's **atmosphere**, especially near the North
Pole and the South Pole. This colorful glow is
called an aurora.

Solar Eclipse

The Moon is much smaller than the Sun. It seems as big because it is much closer to Earth. Sometimes, the Moon moves between Earth and the Sun. It hides the Sun. This is called a solar eclipse.

A solar eclipse happens when the Moon is between Earth and the Sun.

During an eclipse, we can see the Sun's **atmosphere**. It looks like a bright **halo** around the Moon.

Never look right at the Sun during an eclipse. The sunlight can hurt your eyes. It can even make you blind.

Day and Night

The Sun shines all the time, but you only see it during the day. It seems to disappear at night.

Earth is always spinning like a top. It makes one spin every 24 hours. When a place on Earth spins to face the Sun, it is in daylight. When that place spins away from the Sun, it is in night.

When the part of Earth you live on faces the Sun, you have daylight.

Sun and Life

The Sun gives us light and heat. It warms all living things on Earth. The sun also gives plants the light they need to make food and grow. People and animals eat some of these plants.

Plants need light from the Sun to make food and grow.

People eat plants that need sunlight to grow.

Without the Sun, there would be no life on Earth. No plants or animals would have food without light.

Birth and Death of the Sun

The Sun was born about 5 billion years ago. It will burn for about 5 billion years more. Then it will die out, and it will leave a shining circle of gas called a nebula.

Each of the reddish spots in the sky is a nebula.

A nebula is made by a dying star.

Some of the gas that the Sun leaves behind may help form a new star. That new star might even become the center of a new solar system.

Glossary

atmosphere layer of gases around the Sun and each of the planets

energy power that makes heat and sometimes electricity

halo ring of light around an object.

planet One of nine huge, ball-shaped objects that circle the Sun.

solid Hard. Not a liquid or gas.

surface Outside layer of something.

More Books to Read

Berger, Barbara. *When the Sun Rose.* New York: Putnam, 1990.

Daly, Niki. *Why the Sun and Moon Live in the Sky.* New York: Lothrop, 1994.

Ginsburg, Mirra. *Where Does the Sun Go at Night?* New York: Greenwillow, 1980.

Harrison, David. *Wake Up! Sun!* New York: Random Books for Young Readers, 1986.

Index